CAMPAIGN
FOR HUMAN
DEVELOPMEN
**The Catholic Church Working to End
Poverty and Injustice in America.**

MW01610563

Way of the Cross

Toward Justice and Peace

Faith and Human Development Series

United States Catholic Conference • Washington, D.C.

In its formal 1997 planning document, as approved by the general membership of the National Conference of Catholic Bishops, the Campaign for Human Development (CHD) was authorized "to develop relevant materials on social justice issues in order to raise the consciousness of parishioners." This document was prepared under that authorization. The specific text was approved by the Most Rev. Ricardo Ramírez, CSB, chairman of the USCC CHD committee, and was authorized for publication by the undersigned.

Monsignor Dennis M. Schnurr
General Secretary, NCCB/USCC

Prepared for the Campaign for Human Development by Bill Appleby Purcell, education specialist.

Illustration by Patrick M. Birge.

Photo credits:
p. 2: Dale G. Folstad, CNS.
p. 3: Les Fetchko, CNS.
p. 4: Michael R. Hoyt, CNS.
p. 5: CHD.
p. 6: Karen Callaway, CHD.
p. 7: Cleo Freelance Photo, CNS.
p. 8: Dave Vaughn, CHD.
p. 9: Sheree Tucker, CHD.
p. 10: Jim Whitmer Photography.
p. 11: Bild Sivovic, CNS.
p. 12: Julia Dean and Associates.
p. 13: Secretariat for Latin America.
p. 14: Dave Swan, CNS.
p. 15: Michael R. Hoyt, CNS.
p. 16: CHD.

First Printing, March 1998

ISBN 1-57455-235-X

Introduction

Through the traditional devotion of the stations of the cross, Catholics are provided with a spiritual means to follow in the footsteps of Jesus Christ. Jesus suffered for the sins of the world. Today, Christ's suffering continues through the cries of the thousands of men, women, and children who are abandoned and abused, ill and without homes. The cry of Jesus on the cross reveals his solidarity with all of those who are abandoned. God enacts the ultimate preferential option with the poor through this experience of the cross.

Throughout the history of our Church, Catholic women and men have followed the path of Jesus and walked the way of the cross themselves. Many died young; some after years of being witnesses of God's love. This *Way of the Cross: Toward Justice and Peace* follows the final journey of Jesus as shown in Scripture (the words of Jesus are in bold) and highlights those who walked in his footprints. These saintly people, from many walks of life, reveal to us that the power of faith can overcome death and lead us to resurrection.

The Campaign for Human Development (CHD) is a concrete expression of the Catholic Church's belief in the resurrection. Addressing the root causes of poverty in the United States through providing funds to self-help, community organizations and through transformative education, CHD gives life to the messages of justice and hope, the core of Catholic teaching.

May this resource assist you on your journey to follow the way of Jesus Christ.

FIRST STATION:
Jesus Is Condemned to Death

As soon as morning came, the chief priests with the elders and the scribes, that is, the whole Sanhedrin, held a council. They bound Jesus, led him away, and handed him over to Pilate (Mk 15:1).

Pilate said to them, "Then what shall I do with Jesus called Messiah?" They all said, "Let him be crucified!" But he said, "Why? What evil has he done?" They only shouted the louder, "Let him be crucified!" When Pilate saw that he was not succeeding at all, but that a riot was breaking out instead, he took water and washed his hands in the sight of the crowd. . . . Then he released Barabbas to them, but after he had Jesus scourged, he handed him over to be crucified (Mt 27:22-26).

Jesus Continues to Be Condemned to Death

Maximilian Kolbe, a Polish Franciscan priest, was imprisoned during World War II in Auschwitz, a Nazi concentration camp. In 1941 he exchanged his life for another, by volunteering to take the place of a young father condemned to starve to death. Two years earlier, Maximilian had predicted his torture and death when speaking to fellow Franciscan community members.

The third stage of my life will be my lot shortly. It will be one of suffering. But by whom, where, how, and in what form this suffering will come, is known only to the Immaculate Mother.

Words of Jesus

Watch out for yourselves. They will hand you over to the courts. You will be beaten in synagogues. You will be arraigned before governors and kings because of me, as a witness before them (Mk 13:9).

SECOND STATION:
Jesus Takes Up His Cross

Then the soldiers of the governor took Jesus inside the praetorium and gathered the whole cohort around him. They stripped off his clothes and threw a scarlet military cloak about him. Weaving a crown out of thorns, they placed it on his head, and a reed in his right hand. And kneeling before him, they mocked him, saying, "Hail, King of the Jews!" They spat upon him and took the reed and kept striking him on the head. And when they had mocked him, they stripped him of the cloak, dressed him in his own clothes, and led him off to crucify him (Mt 27:27-31).

Jesus Continues to Carry the Cross

Franz Jäger-stätter was an uneducated farmer from a small village in Austria, a husband, and a father of three children. He was convinced that it would be immoral for him to serve in the Nazi army during World War II, so he refused. Franz was imprisoned and after a military trial, he was beheaded in August 1943. The night before his execution, the words Franz told his chaplain sealed his fate.

> I cannot and may not take an oath in favor of a government that is fighting an unjust war. . . . I believe it cannot possibly be a crime or a sin for a Catholic simply to refuse the [Nazi government] even though he knows this will mean certain death. For is it not more Christian to offer oneself as a victim right away rather than first to murder others . . . just to prolong one's own life a little while?

Words of Jesus

Whoever wishes to come after me must deny himself, take up his cross, and follow me (Mt 16:24).

THIRD STATION:
Jesus Falls the First Time

So they took Jesus, and carrying the cross by himself he went out to what is called the Place of the Skull, in Hebrew, Golgotha (Jn 19:16-17).

After withdrawing about a stone's throw from them and kneeling, he prayed, saying, **"Father, if you are willing, take this cup away from me; still, not my will but yours be done"** (Lk 22:41-42).

Jesus Is Still Falling

Sister Thea Bowman, a member of the Franciscan Sisters of the Perpetual Adoration, continued in her mission as a gospel singer and evangelist despite battling cancer. During her illness that bound her to a wheelchair, she maintained a grueling schedule of lectures and singing performances designed to raise awareness and appreciation of African American Catholic culture. Two weeks before her death on March 30, 1990, Sister Thea continued to offer hope and courage.

> I've always asked God for the grace to live until I die. . . . To the suffering I say: "Try to reach out to others. Try to let people know how much you love them. Try to maintain a sense of humor and laughter in your life."

Words of Jesus

Blessed are you when they insult you and persecute you and utter every kind of evil against you [falsely] because of me (Mt 5:11).

FOURTH STATION:
Jesus Meets His Mother

There were also women looking on from a distance. Among them were Mary Magdalene, Mary the mother of the younger James and of Joses, and Salome. These women had followed him when he was in Galilee and ministered to him. There were also many other women who had come up with him to Jerusalem (Mk 15:40-41).

Standing by the cross of Jesus were his mother and his mother's sister, Mary the wife of Clopas, and Mary of Magdala. When Jesus saw his mother and the disciple there whom he loved, he said to his mother, **"Woman, behold, your son"** (Jn 19:25-26).

God chose the foolish of the world to shame the wise, and God chose the weak of the world to shame the strong (1 Cor 1:27).

Jesus Continues to Meet His Mother, Mary

Kateri Tekakwitha, often called the Lily of the Mohawks, survived a smallpox epidemic that killed her family and disfigured her face. Jesuit missionaries placed her in the care of Anastasia Tegonhatsiongo, whom Kateri came to look upon as her mother. Devoting her short life to caring for the sick and aged, Kateri died in 1680 at the age of twenty-four.

One week after Kateri died she appeared to her adopted mother, Anastasia. Kateri stood in a light holding a cross. She said that the cross had been the source of her happiness during her time in the world and that Anastasia should look to the cross as her inspiration, too.

Words of Jesus

Forgive us our debts, as we forgive our debtors (Mt 6:12).

FIFTH STATION:
Simon of Cyrene Helps Jesus

As they led him away they took hold of a certain Simon, a Cyrenian, who was coming in from the country; and after laying the cross on him, they made him carry it behind Jesus (Lk 23:26).

Simon the Cyrenian Continues to Offer Help

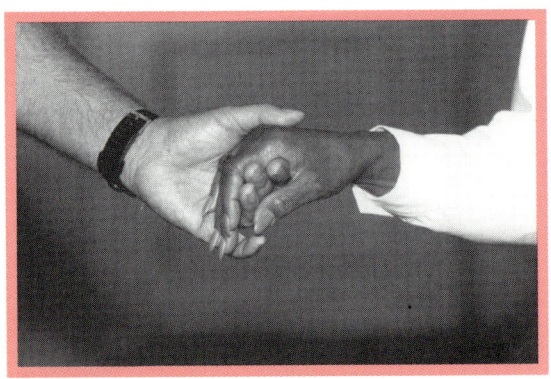

Thomas More, Lord Chancellor of England under King Henry VIII, was one of the outstanding lay people of his time. In 1534 he was imprisoned in the Tower of London because he refused to give absolute allegiance to the king, giving his absolute allegiance to Christ instead. Thomas was tried, convicted of treason, and beheaded after fifteen months in prison. His letters from prison reflect his view that a believing Christian must be an active Christian.

O Lord, give us the grace to read or hear the Gospel of your bitter passion not with our eyes or our ears in the manner of a past time, but that it may so sink into our hearts that it stretches to the everlasting profit of our souls. . . . Though faith is the first gate into heaven, the person who stands at the gate and does not step forward in the way of good works will not enter into where the reward is.

Words of Jesus

You know that the rulers of the Gentiles lord it over them, and the great ones make their authority over them felt. But it shall not be so among you. Rather, whoever wishes to be great among you shall be your servant (Mt 20:25-26).

SIXTH STATION:
Veronica Wipes the Face of Jesus

A woman suffering hemorrhages for twelve years came up behind him and touched the tassel on his cloak. She said to herself, "If only I can touch his cloak, I shall be cured." Jesus turned around and saw her, and said, **"Courage, daughter! Your faith has saved you."** And from that hour the woman was cured (Mt 9:20-22).

Veronica Is Still Wiping the Face of Jesus

Jean Donovan, a lay missionary in El Salvador, was raped and killed during the Salvadoran civil war in 1980 along with fellow American women, Dorothy Kazel, Maura Clarke, and Ita Ford. Two weeks before she was killed, Jean wrote to a friend.

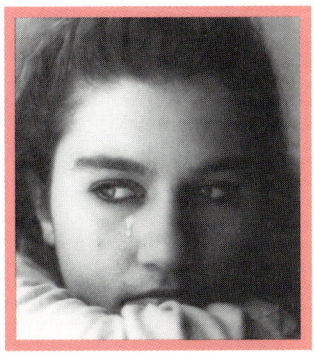

Several times I have decided to leave El Salvador. I almost could except for the children, the poor, bruised victims of this insanity. Who would care for them? Whose heart would be so staunch as to favor the reasonable thing in a sea of tears and helplessness? Not mine, dear friend, not mine.

Words of Jesus

You are the light of the world. . . . Your light must shine before others, that they may see your good deeds and glorify your heavenly Father (Mt 5:14, 16).

SEVENTH STATION:
Jesus Falls a Second Time

If God is for us, who can be against us? [God] who did not spare his own Son but handed him over for us all, how will he not also give us everything else along with him? (Rom 8:31-32)

My foes all whisper against me;
    they imagine the worst about me:
I have a deadly disease, they say;
    I will never rise from my sickbed. . . .
But you, LORD, have mercy and raise me up
    that I may repay them as they deserve (Ps 41:8-9, 11).

Jesus Falls Again and Again

Dorothy Day, co-founder of the Catholic Worker movement, was a journalist and a pacifist. She was a leader in the Catholic peace movement until her death in 1980. Dorothy was also a leading voice in support of the causes of the poor and dispossessed. Her commitment to social justice, strengthened by her deep religious faith, is evident by her six imprisonments for civil rights. During one of Dorothy's imprisonments, she described her feelings of loss.

In the cell I lost all feeling of my own identity. That I would be free after thirty days meant nothing to me. I would never be free again. Solitude and hunger and weariness of spirit—these sharpened my perceptions so that I suffered not only my own sorrow but the sorrows of those about me. I was no longer a young girl . . . I was the oppressed.

Words of Jesus

They will seize and persecute you, they will hand you over to the synagogues and to prisons, and they will have you led before kings and governors because of my name (Lk 21:12).

EIGHTH STATION:
Jesus Speaks to the Women of Jerusalem

A large crowd of people followed Jesus, including many women who mourned and lamented him. Jesus turned to them and said, "**Daughters of Jerusalem, do not weep for me; weep instead for yourselves and for your children, for indeed, the days are coming when people will say, 'Blessed are the barren, the wombs that never bore and the breasts that never nursed.' At that time people will say to the mountains, 'Fall upon us!' and to the hills, 'Cover us!' for if these things are done when the wood is green what will happen when it is dry?**" (Lk 23:27-31)

Women Still Weep for Jesus

St. Teresa of Avila, the first woman doctor of the Church, was a mystic and founder in the sixteenth century of the Discalced Carmelites. Her writings reveal her understanding of the struggle of Christ.

One day my Lord said to me: "Believe me, my daughter, trials are the heaviest for those my Father loves the best. Trials are God's measure of love. How could I better demonstrate my love for you than by desiring for you what I desired for myself?"

To be truly spiritual is to make ourselves slaves of God branded with the cross. God can give no greater grace than to give us a life such as was led by Jesus.

Words of Jesus

Father, forgive them, they know not what they do (Lk 23:34).

NINTH STATION:
Jesus Falls the Third Time

My iniquities overwhelm me,
  a burden beyond my strength (Ps 38:5).

Jesus Keeps Falling Again and Again

Cardinal Joseph Bernardin, born in South Carolina, became a priest for the Diocese of Charleston before becoming an auxiliary bishop of Atlanta and archbishop of Cincinnati and then of Chicago. He chaired the U.S. bishops' committee that drafted a pastoral letter on war and peace. The cardinal was a constant and staunch defender of the sanctity and dignity of human life at all stages from conception to natural death. In a well-known speech he delivered at Fordham University, he articulated the "seamless garment" metaphor for the consistent ethic of life. Cardinal Bernardin, respected for his spiritual leadership, died in November 1996 of pancreatic cancer. He expressed his sentiments while dying in his memoir, *The Gift of Peace*.

> In my homily for the liturgy of my solemn installation as Seventh Archbishop of Chicago, I had reminded the congregation . . . that Jesus, the Good Shepherd, the model for all my ministry
>
>> is one who lays down his life for his people. Some live this call literally, shedding their blood as martyrs. Others live it in the unstinting giving of their time, their energy, their very selves to those they have been called to serve. Whatever the future holds for me, I pledge this day to live as a good shepherd who willingly lays down his life for you.
>
> The words are simple and direct, and I meant with all my being what I said.

Words of Jesus

When they lead you away and hand you over, do not worry beforehand about what you are to say. But say whatever will be given to you at that hour. For it will not be you who are speaking but the holy Spirit (Mk 13:11).

TENTH STATION:
Jesus Is Stripped of His Clothes

When the soldiers had crucified Jesus, they took his clothes and divided them into four shares, a share for each soldier. They also took his tunic, but the tunic was seamless, woven in one piece from the top down. So they said to one another, "Let's not tear it, but cast lots for it to see whose it will be," in order that the passage of scripture might be fulfilled [that says]:

"They divided my garments among them,
and for my vesture they cast lots." (Jn 19:23-24)

Jesus Is Still Stripped Naked Today

Joan of Arc, the patroness of France, was an illiterate peasant teenager who led French troops against English forces in 1430. She was taken prisoner and held in jail for about a year. Joan was tried as a heretic, sentenced to death, excommunicated, and at the age of nineteen, she was burned at the stake. At her trial she defended her faith.

All my words and deeds are in the hands of God. With regard to them I bow to Him. And I swear to you that I do not want to do anything contrary to the Christian faith, and if I have done or said anything . . . , I do not want to defend it, but will repudiate it.
If I am condemned—and I see the fire lit, the wood made ready, and the scaffold—and when I am in the fire, I shall not say differently from what I have already said.

Words of Jesus

Behold, I am sending you like sheep in the midst of wolves; so be shrewd as serpents and simple as doves. But beware of people, for they will hand you over to courts and scourge you in their synagogues, and you will be led before governors and kings for my sake as a witness before them and the pagans (Mt 10:16-18).

ELEVENTH STATION:
Jesus Is Nailed to the Cross

It was nine o'clock in the morning when they crucified him. . . . With him they crucified two revolutionaries, one on his right and one on his left (Mk 15:25-27).

Live in love, as Christ loved us and handed himself over for us as a sacrificial offering to God (Eph 5:2).

Jesus Continues to Be Nailed to the Cross

Isaac Jogues was a French Jesuit missionary to North America in the seventeenth century. He and his companions were tortured by members of the Mohawk tribe in New York. He survived but was made a slave to a Mohawk woman. Isaac escaped and  returned to France. When he came back to America in 1646 to pursue his missionary work among the Mohawks, he was murdered by an Iroquois warrior. His tortures were so brutal that he wrote his reports to his superiors in Latin, so that the common person would not be horrified by the accounts.

I, who was the last, and therefore more exposed to these beatings, fell, midway in the journey which we were obliged to make to a hill, on which they had created a stage. I thought that I must die there, because I neither could nor cared to arise. What I suffered is known to One for whose love and cause it is a pleasant and glorious thing to suffer.

Words of Jesus

Amen, amen, I say to you, whoever believes in me will do the works that I do, and will do greater ones than these, because I am going to the Father (Jn 14:12).

TWELFTH STATION:
Jesus Dies on the Cross

At noon darkness came over the whole land until three in the afternoon. And at three o'clock Jesus cried out in a loud voice, *"Eloi, Eloi, lema sabachthani?"* which is translated, **"My God, my God, why have you forsaken me?"** . . . Jesus gave a loud cry and breathed his last (Mk 15:33-34, 37).

Jesus Still Dies on the Cross Each Day

Oscar Romero, archbishop of San Salvador in El Salvador, was assassinated while celebrating the eucharist in a hospital chapel. He was targeted because of his stance of defending the poor and powerless against the unjust institutions of his country. In the last homily he gave in that final eucharist, Oscar associated his life and death with Christ's.

This holy Mass is clearly an act of faith. . . . In the chalice, the wine is transformed into the blood that was the price of salvation. This body broken and this blood shed for human beings encourage us to give our body and blood up to suffering and pain, as Christ did— not for self, but to bring justice and peace to our people.

Words of Jesus

You have heard that it was said, "You shall love your neighbor and hate your enemy." But I say to you, love your enemies, and pray for those who persecute you (Mt 5:43-44).

THIRTEENTH STATION:
Jesus Is Removed from the Cross

Joseph of Arimathea, a distinguished member of the council, who was himself awaiting the kingdom of God, came and courageously went to Pilate and asked for the body of Jesus. . . . [Pilate] gave the body to Joseph. Having bought a linen cloth, he took him down, wrapped him in the linen cloth and laid him in a tomb (Mk 15:43, 45-46).

The Mother of God Continues to Weep Over Her Children

Mother Jones, a Catholic immigrant from Canada, was a mother widowed by a yellow fever epidemic. Mary Harris Jones devoted her life to the American labor movement during its early years. She was subjected to numerous arrests, vicious attacks on her reputation, harassment by militia guards, and the wrath of public officials, corporate executives, and union leaders. Despite all of this, she persisted in helping laborers to secure a fundamental human right—the right to form a union. When

she was eighty, and still organizing, she testified before a congressional committee that asked her where she lived. She responded

> I live in the United States, but I do not know exactly in what place, because I am always in the fight against oppression, and wherever a fight is going on I have to jump there, and sometimes I am in Washington, sometimes in Pennsylvania, sometimes in Arizona, sometimes in Texas, and sometimes up in Minnesota, so that I really have no particular residence.

Words of Jesus

Foxes have dens and birds of the sky have nests, but the Son of Man has nowhere to rest his head (Mt 8:20).

FOURTEENTH STATION:
Jesus Is Placed in the Tomb

Taking the body, Joseph wrapped it [in] clean linen and laid it in his new tomb that he had hewn in the rock. Then he rolled a huge stone across the entrance to the tomb and departed. But Mary Magdalene and the other Mary remained sitting there, facing the tomb (Mt 27:59-61).

Jesus Is Still Being Placed in the Tomb

Tom Dooley, a Catholic doctor originally from St. Louis, worked tirelessly to bring medical care to refugees in Southeast Asia during the 1950s and 1960s while battling cancer himself. The month before he died, Tom wrote a letter acknowledging his pain. In the same letter, he wrote of the peace he found resting in God.

But yet a milder storm of peace gathers in my heart. What seems unpossessable, I can possess. What seems unfathomable, I fathom. What is unutterable, I can utter. Because I can pray, I can communicate. How do people endure anything on earth if they cannot have God?

Words of Jesus

This is my commandment: love one another as I love you. No one has greater love than this, to lay down one's life for one's friends (Jn 15:12-13).

FIFTEENTH STATION:
Resurrection of Jesus

Why do you seek the living one among the dead? He is not here, but he has been raised (Lk 24:5-6).

So whoever is in Christ is a new creation: the old things have passed away; behold, new things have come (2 Cor 5:17).

The Resurrection Continues to Occur

The Campaign for Human Development (CHD), the Catholic Church's domestic anti-poverty program, is a concrete way the Church in the United States lives out the resurrection experience of Christ. CHD emphasizes empowerment and participation for the poor by funding more than three thousand self-help projects developed by grassroots groups of poor persons. The projects' successes and the relationships developed have significantly changed the lives of the poor in our country.

Words of Jesus

Blessed are the poor in spirit,
    for theirs is the kingdom of heaven.
Blessed are they who mourn,
    for they will be comforted.
Blessed are the meek,
    for they will inherit the land.
Blessed are they who hunger and thirst for righteousness,
    for they will be satisfied.
Blessed are the merciful,
    for they will be shown mercy.
Blessed are the clean of heart,
    for they will see God.
Blessed are the peacemakers,
    for they will be called children of God.
Blessed are they who are persecuted for the sake of righteousness,
    for theirs is the kingdom of heaven (Mt 5:3-10).

Acknowledgments

Grateful acknowledgment is made to the following for permission to reprint material.

Cardinal Joseph Bernardin excerpt from *The Gift of Peace: Personal Reflections by Joseph Cardinal Bernardin,* copyright © 1997 by Catholic Bishop of Chicago, a Corporation Sole. Used by permission of Loyola Press. All rights reserved.

Dorothy Day excerpt from *Loaves and Fishes,* copyright © 1963 by Dorothy Day. Used by permission of HarperCollins Publishers. All rights reserved.

Franz Jägerstätter excerpt from *In Solitary Witness* by Gordon C. Zahn, copyright © 1964. Used by permission of the author. All rights reserved.

Maximilian Kolbe excerpt from *Ten Christians* by Boniface Hanley, OFM, copyright © 1979 by St. Anthony's Guild, Paterson, NJ 07509. Used by permission of Ave Maria Press, Notre Dame, IN 46556. All rights reserved.

Mother Jones excerpt from *Mother Jones Speaks,* copyright © 1983 by Philip S. Foner. Used by permission of Pathfinder Press. All rights reserved.

Oscar Romero excerpt from *A Martyr's Message of Hope,* copyright © 1981. Used by permission of Sheed & Ward, 115 E. Armour Blvd., Kansas City, MO 64111. All rights reserved.

Scripture texts used in this work are taken from the *New American Bible,* copyright © 1991, 1986, and 1970 by the Confraternity of Christian Doctrine, Washington, D.C. 20017 and are used by permission of copyright owner. All rights reserved.

Sr. Thea Bowman excerpt "Sister Thea Bowman: On the Road to Glory," March 30, 1990, reprinted with permission from *U.S. Catholic,* published by Claretian Publications, 205 W. Monroe Street, Chicago, IL 60606. All rights reserved.

St. Teresa of Avila excerpt from *Let Nothing Disturb You: A Journey to the Center of the Soul With Teresa of Avila* by John Kirvan, copyright © 1996 by Quest Associates. Used by permission of Ave Maria Press, Notre Dame, IN 46556. All rights reserved.

Thomas More excerpt from *A Book for All Seasons* by E. E. Reynolds, copyright © 1979. Used by permission of Templegate Publishers (www.templegate.com). All rights reserved.

Tom Dooley excerpt from *No Strangers to Violence, No Strangers to Love* by Boniface F. Hanley, OFM, copyright © 1983. Used by permission of the author. All rights reserved.

Other References

Kateri Tekakwitha reference from *Saints in the Making* by Felicity O'Brien, copyright © 1988.

Every effort has been made to contact the publishers/copyright owners of the following excerpts. If any omission or infringement of copyright has occurred, amendment will be made upon notification.

Isacc Jogues excerpt from *Saints of the Americas* by Rev. M. A. Habig, OFM, copyright © 1974. All rights reserved.

Jean Donovan excerpt from *Salvador Witness* by Ana Carrigan, copyright © 1984. All rights reserved.

Joan of Arc excerpt from *Joan of Arc* by John Holland Smith, copyright © 1973. All rights reserved.